{ CITIESCAPE }

HONG KONG*

{ CITIESCAPE }

ANDREW BURKE

CONTENTS*

VITAL STATS*

{ }

NAME Hong Kong **AKA** The City of Lights
DATE OF BIRTH 206 BC when the Eastern
Han Dynasty ruled; China ceded the island to
Great Britain in 1842 and got back control in 1997
HEIGHT 33m **SIZE** 1103 sq km
ADDRESS China, Special Administrative Region
POPULATION 7.2 million

7.

PEOPLE*

{ ***HONG KONG MIGHT SELL ITSELF AS 'ASIA'S WORLD CITY', BUT THE NUMBERS SUGGEST ITS SOUL IS OVERWHELMINGLY CANTONESE.** About 95% of the population is ethnic Chinese, mostly from Guangzhou, and 60% were born in the territory, leaving Hong Kongers feeling different, somehow, from their mainland cousins. }

PERHAPS IT'S the years of British-sponsored devotion to the free market, or maybe just the political freedom to be Chinese – work hard and make a profit – but in Hong Kong there is more faith in capitalism than in the traditional religions of Buddhism, Taoism and Confucianism. Economic necessity is a big influence on the average Hong Kong family. Couples with office jobs who live in a modest apartment with their one or two kids are the norm. Due to the high costs of raising children the birthrate has fallen from three children per family in 1980 to just 0.9 in 2005. Increasingly, the city's wealth and high standards of education are translating into a greater appreciation of outsiders and a growing social awareness, making Hong Kongers more interesting people to be around.

9.

ANATOMY*

{ *HONG KONG IS MORE THAN A CITY OF SKYSCRAPERS. SPREADING ACROSS 235 ISLANDS AND A SMALL CHUNK OF SOUTHERN CHINA,** almost 90% of the city is grassy hills, mountains and subtropical jungles with nary an apartment block in sight. Despite all this open space, only 2% of the land is cultivated – it's cheaper to import food from the mainland. }

THE HEART OF the city is Victoria Harbour, a frenetic playground for ferries, sampans and the enormous container ships that dock at the world's busiest shipping port. On either side of the harbour are Hong Kong Island and Kowloon, where forests of concrete apartment towers are home to about half the population.

THERE'S NOWHERE to park cars in Hong Kong, so few people own them. Instead, they rely on the ultra-efficient MTR railway, bracingly cold buses, the iconic Star Ferry and the longest pedestrian escalator on earth. Add Hong Kong's much-lauded airport and you have a transport system that often leaves you smiling in appreciation – a rarity indeed.

PERSON ALITY*

{ *** IF HONG KONG WAS A PERSON, SHE'D BE A DIFFICULT WOMAN TO UNDERSTAND. SHE'D BE HIGH MAINTENANCE AND HIGH REWARD.** She'd be constantly changing, without losing touch with her heritage. She'd be well educated but always willing to learn more. She'd be superstitious but scientific when she wanted to be. She'd love dim sum and pizza too. She'd be exotic, but familiar; a gambler, but one who always knows the odds; immaculately dressed, but knowing how to let her hair down. And even when she stayed out late she'd be at work on time. She'd be all these things, she'd be a contradiction and a conundrum. But more than anything, she'd be fun and you'd always want to be around her. }

TO UNDERSTAND HOW Hong Kong acquired such a complex and seductive personality it's necessary to look at its past. Though the long British colonial era was crucial, it's the decade since handover that has truly built the city's character. Hong Kongers never felt part of Britain, but it wasn't until China resumed control in 1997 that they realised they didn't really feel part of China either. It was as if the penny had finally dropped – they might be Chinese people living the vague idea of 'one country, two systems', but they are also Hong Kongers, and that is its own identity.

THE FOUNDATIONS on which that unique identity is built are everywhere. Some are almost trivial, such as when a British administrator arranged for the sign for tiny Alexander Street in Mid-Levels to be painted. The Chinese painter began at the wrong end and the result was 'Rednaxela', which it remains to this day.

OTHERS ARE LESS visible but have been critical in shaping Hong Kong's personality: a seven-year economic downturn, avian flu and SARS are three examples. Then there's the considerable financial help China provided when it unleashed hordes of mainland tourists on the city. Not surprisingly, Hong Kongers embraced the mainlanders and their dollars with open arms, and they began to understand that China has no intention of changing Hong Kong because it's too busy reinventing itself in Hong Kong's image. Talk about affirming.

DESPITE ALL the changes, the world's view of Hong Kong remains steeped in stereo-types. A couple of such misconceptions you can toss out immediately are that it's just a concrete jungle and that it's as exotic as a Big Mac. The vast majority of Hong Kong is actually easily accessible green zones – knowing that escape is as near as the Star Ferry is central to the city's psyche. And while the glittering towers might look familiar, the temples, tai chi and burning 'hell money' probably won't. The city's Chinese roots run deep.

FLICK THROUGH Hong Kong's snapshots over the chapters that follow and explore something of the city's personality. It's unique. It's addictive. It's Hong Kong… and it's better than ever.

HYPER KINETIC*

{ ***THERE'S AN ENERGY ABOUT HONG KONG THAT'S HARD TO DEFINE BUT IMPOSSIBLE TO IGNORE.** No matter the time, no matter the day, there's always something going on. It's the supreme 24-hour city. }

TO UNDERSTAND this endless energy, start by looking at the people. With their relentless 24/7 work ethic, Hong Kongers are always trying to stay ahead, driven by an unshakeable belief that prosperity comes from hard graft and shrewd judgment. If something doesn't work, the next opportunity is just around the corner. If it does work, then there's some way of improving it… and the buzz feeds on itself.

THERE'S A SWAGGER in this city's hyperkinetic step, a renewed optimism among the punters striding into Happy Valley Racecourse, the tai tais (wealthy women of leisure) shopping in Causeway Bay and the Chinese and expats out on the pull in Lan Kwai Fong. The confidence is reflected in a new sophistication, seen in the growing appreciation of the arts. Galleries seem to open every week and art has become almost as hip as fashion.

17.

And the live music scene is no longer limited to impromptu performances by Melvis the Elvis impersonator, as much as we love him.

ALL THIS HUMAN drive manifests itself in the physical blocks on which Hong Kong is built. The celebrated skyline and countless apartment buildings are most obvious, but they'd be nothing without the infrastructure that serves them. One key is the super-punctual MTR train system, in which your mobile phone works no matter how far underground you are. And the world's busiest container port keeps the goods moving and the money flowing.

WITH EVERYONE living, working and travelling in such close proximity, it's little wonder Hong Kongers know how to let off steam. Horse racing is a favourite release in this gambling-mad city, and once the neon begins to burn Wan Chai, SoHo and Lan Kwai Fong start pumping. These entertainment districts also reflect Hong Kong's endless reinvention. Not all that long ago SoHo (aka South of Hollywood Road) and Lan Kwai Fong were poor Chinese neighbourhoods. Today, they are barely recognisable. Even Wan Chai, so long a seedy den of iniquity, is beginning to flirt with gentrification.

IN FACT there is so much change in Hong Kong that it's almost impossible to keep up. No matter how many times you visit, there is always something new. Stores, restaurants, bars, nightclubs, karaoke joints, galleries and skyscrapers are the obvious ones; a reclaimed piece of harbour and a thriving protest culture are a little more surprising. And with the economy booming and so many mainland Chinese tourists flooding into the city, the changes are set to continue apace.

18.

SKY HIGH*

{ *** IT WOULDN'T BE HONG KONG WITHOUT THE TOWERS. RISING FROM THE EDGE OF VICTORIA HARBOUR** and climbing steeply up the hills of Victoria Peak, Hong Kong's hectic skyline of glass, concrete and gaudy neon is a metaphor for the city's endless energy – and its ability to reinvent itself. }

AMONG ALL the offices and apartments are some towers that truly stand out. The newest and tallest is IFC 2, which looms over Central like super-sized hair clippers – it's known colloquially as 'Sir YK Pao's Erection', a reference to the owner of the company that built it.

THE BANK OF China Tower is another landmark. It was opened on 8 August 1988 (8/8/88), the luckiest day for, well, a century, but any Hong Konger can tell you it projects terrible feng shui. Its four triangular prisms are negative symbols: they're the opposite of circles and thus contradict all that circles suggest – money, prosperity and perfection.

20.

PEDESTRIAN PLEASURES *

{ **THE PULSE OF THE CITY IS LOUD IN LAN KWAI FONG, FOUR NARROW STREETS IN CENTRAL THAT ARE A MELTING POT OF ETHNICITIES,** cuisines, neon signs and grotesque jello shots. Though it's less than 100 metres from one of the busiest intersections in Hong Kong, the area was a poor Chinese neighbourhood until the early 1990s. In the years since there have been constant nips and tucks and several major face-lifts and the area has become the premier clubbing and drinking district in Hong Kong. }

LAN KWAI FONG is busy every night, and on weekends goes off like the proverbial box of Chinese firecrackers. The street, the bars and the restaurants are packed with the young, hip and cashed up, a mix of expats, tourists and upwardly mobile Chinese, all enjoying a little pub-crawling. It's an expensive area to party in, though, so much of the crowd spills over into nearby 'Rat Alley' for cheap and excellent Malaysian food.

KOWLOON HAS a Lan Kwai Fong equivalent, up along Knutsford Terrace, but it's just a bit tackier, less imaginative and more run-down.

23.

A DAY AT THE RACES*

{ *FEW ACTIVITIES CAPTURE THE HONG KONG OBSESSION WITH LUCK AND HONG KONGERS' WILLINGNESS TO GAMBLE ON IT MORE THAN THE HORSE RACES. }

There are about 80 meetings a year at two racecourses: the classic, sloping Happy Valley track on Hong Kong Island with a capacity of 35,000, and the newer and larger Sha Tin course in the New Territories, accommodating 85,000.

HORSE RACING is one of the few legal forms of gambling and in 2005 more than HK$60 billion was bet on the races. For the many punters who can't afford the trip to the casinos of Macau, watching horse form becomes almost an obsession.

THE RACING SEASON runs from September to June and is hugely popular; the enormous prizes attract the finest trainers and jockeys on earth, plus – if you believe the talk – a fair share of gangsters. Red-letter days at the races include the Chinese New Year races in January; the Hong Kong Derby in March; the Queen Elizabeth II Cup in April; and the rich Hong Kong International Races in December.

ACTION!*

*BOOM! POW! WHAM! CRASH! NO, NOT BATMAN, BUT THE HONG KONG MOVIE SCENE.** The city that gave the world Jackie Chan (who began life as a performer in a local Chinese opera) was for a while the third-largest producer of films on earth, after Bollywood and Hollywood. And while there have been some fine dramas, romances and comedies, it's action that rules here. Check out almost anything with Jackie Chan, or John Woo's *A Better Tomorrow* with its 'bullet ballet' finale, or Tsui Hark's ultimate kung fu flick *Once Upon a Time in China*.

THERE ARE SOME interesting contrasts to Western films in productions like Chan Wui-ngai's *Bet to Basic*, a movie about mah jong featuring sets of tiles with winning combinations that Hong Kongers find riveting. Johnnie To's *Election* is a glimpse into the inner workings and rituals of Triad society, where party leaders and the 'uncles' are involved in a ruthless struggle for ultimate power yet still live with honour within the Triad codes.

26.

ROCKS & ROLLS*

{ *IF YOU COULD SUM UP THE MANY EXCESSES OF HONG KONG IN A SINGLE PERSON, SHE WOULD BE A TAI TAI.** Tai tai simply means 'Mrs', and strictly speaking every married woman is a tai tai. But in Hong Kong the word is mainly used to refer to the wealthy, pampered wives of successful businessmen. A tai tai's life revolves around lunching with fellow tai tais, taking tea in the trendiest cafés, gossiping on her mobile phone and shopping, shopping, shopping! }

NO SELF-RESPECTING tai tai would go more than a week without unleashing herself and her husband's credit card on the most fashionable boutiques. However, no matter how large the credit limit, tai tais love a bargain. So if she's feeling energetic, a raid on the bargain houses of Shenzhen might be in order. Shenzhen straddles the Hong Kong border with China, and was once a tiny fishing village. Now, it's essentially an extended shopping mall of innumerable factory outlets and shops.

29.

PORT OF CALL*

* HONG KONG IS THE WORLD'S LARGEST SHIPPING PORT. DAY AND NIGHT THE CRANES WORK, MOVING GIANT STEEL CONTAINERS here and there like some Legoland of the gods. And despite Hong Kong's economic woes and the emergence of new ports in China, the city has confounded the experts by having consistently rising traffic during recent years. In 2005 the equivalent of more than 10 million 40-foot containers passed through the port, carried by an astonishing 200,000 ocean and river vessels.

HONG KONG offers purpose-built bridges that allow ocean vessel clearance, several typhoon shelters at places like Aberdeen and Cheung Chau, a range of terminals and shipyards, tugs, dredges, floating docks and midstream operations.

31.

KARAOKE CAPITAL*

{ *** FOR AN EXPRESSION OF HONG KONG'S HYPERKINETIC SIDE THAT IS BOTH DISTINCTLY ASIAN AND DELIGHTFULLY UNSELFCONSCIOUS,** look no further than the city's passion for karaoke. No matter how cheesy people from the West think karaoke is, Hong Kongers don't care – they love it. }

ASK ALMOST ANYONE and they'll tell you they're happy to keep turning up to karaoke parties, no matter how mercilessly their friends butcher a favourite song. They get especially excited when the office party is held at a local karaoke megacomplex – listening to your colleague destroy *I Did It My Way* is, it seems, strangely comforting.

MANY BARS AND even restaurants throughout the city have private karaoke rooms, but Causeway Bay is the karaoke capital. The dozens of studios there are temples to the art (or the crime?) and offer copious amounts of food and drink to go with the mikes and terrible videos.

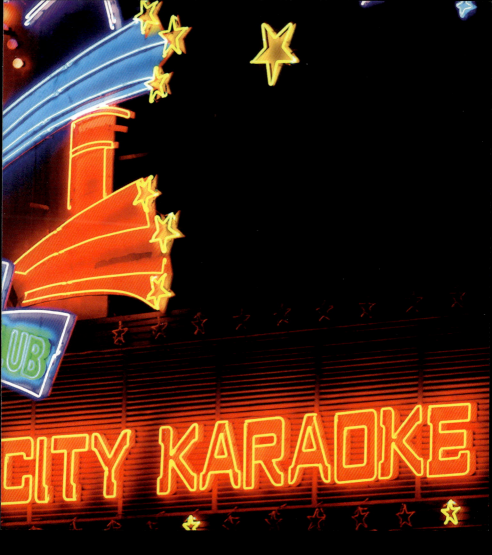

EXOTIC*

* SOME PEOPLE LIKE TO SAY THAT HONG KONG, IN ITS MODERNITY AND RATHER ENTHUSIASTIC EMBRACE of capitalism (to understate things slightly!), has lost its soul. Mercifully, they're wrong. This is a city where the modern mixes shamelessly with the ancient, where people are perfectly happy to burn 'money' for their dead relatives one minute and step inside to resume their game of online poker the next. As you'll have heard and read ad nauseum, Hong Kong is a place where East meets West, but to reduce it to such a tired old cliché is to sell it short.

FOR MORE THAN 150 years Hong Kongers have adopted the aspects of Western culture that suit them best without losing sight of their Eastern heritage. While visitors find much that's familiar in today's Hong Kong, the city is firmly grounded in its Chinese roots. For every McDonalds (and there are more than 200!) there are many more dai pai dong (open-air food stalls) and local restaurants serving Cantonese dishes. People work in towering office blocks – but they've been designed using feng shui principles.

{ And despite laughter from foreigners in the past, Hong Kongers have continued to believe in 'superstitions', consult soothsayers and use traditional medicines. }

THERE IS NO denying that the citizens of Hong Kong live a sort of uber-urban existence, jammed into the city and voraciously consumerist. But partly in reaction to this and to the last decade of rapid globalisation, the city's cultural heritage is being celebrated more than ever. In some cases, as with the super-stylish cheongsams (Chinese traditional dress) from the Shanghai Tang store, the traditional has become the cool. In others, Hong Kongers have simply woken up to the value of their heritage, whether it means money or not. In this city, that is saying a lot.

AS SURPRISING as Hong Kong can be, however, some of the stereotypes ring true. Capitalism is a 'religion' that co-exists fairly harmoniously with more recognised faiths like Buddhism, Taoism and Confucianism. The city is obsessed by 'face' – and not losing face in any transaction or relationship is just about the number-one priority for many Hong Kongers. And while the old chestnut that the city would prefer to shop than pursue the pleasures of the flesh is hard to verify one way or the other, there's a definite correlation between Hong Kong's rapidly rising wealth and its fast-falling birth rate – the median age has risen from 30 in 1989 to almost 40 today.

IT'S THE COMBINATION of all these things, recognisable or unfamiliar, that forms the essence of Hong Kong's very healthy soul.

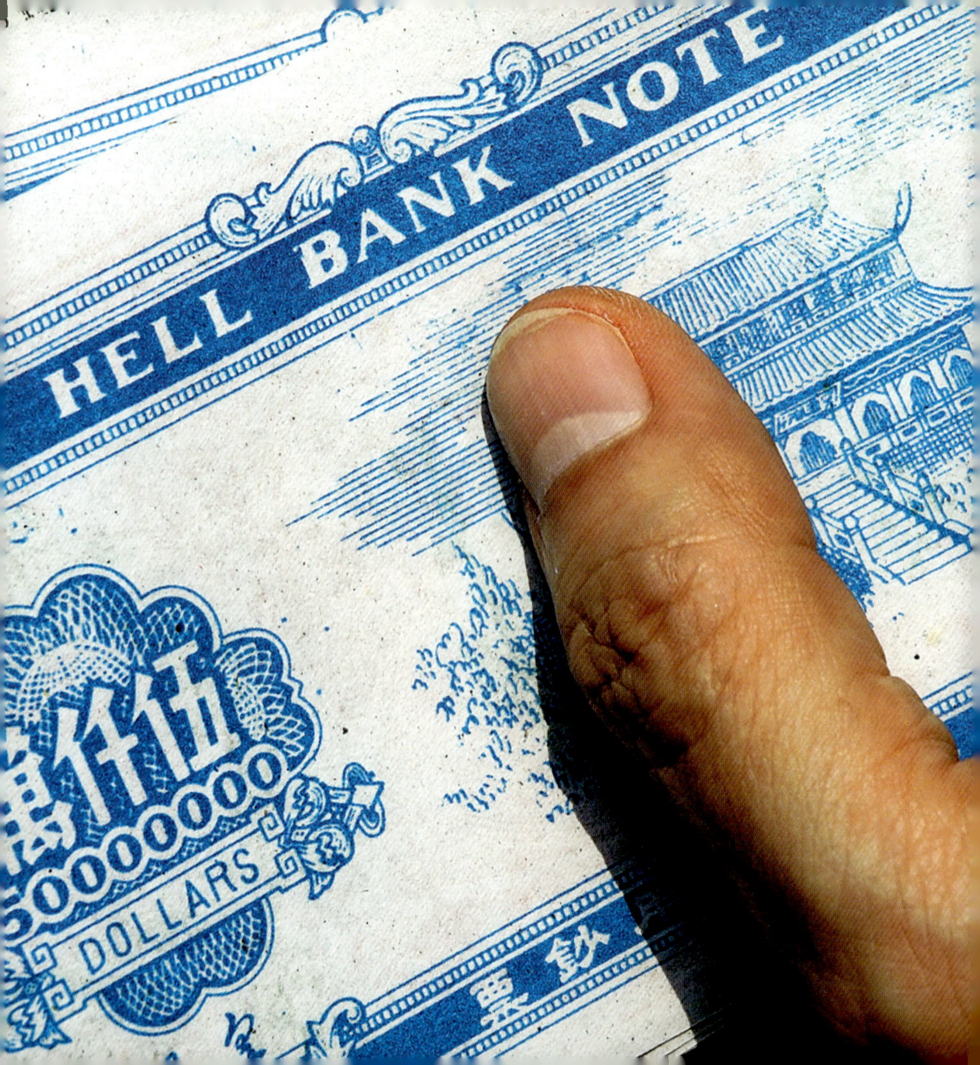
HELL BANK NOTE
伍仟
5000000000
DOLLARS
鈔票

MONEY TO BURN *

{ *THE 'BANK OF HELL' IS BUSY IN HONG KONG. NOTES ARE PRINTED IN ITS NAME BY THE BILLION,** only to be torched to appease the spirits of deceased Hong Kongers. Funerals are often accompanied by bonfires of paper objects representing items the dead would like to take with them into the afterlife. These range from the modest, such as gold watches and clothes, to papier-mâché mansions, Rolls-Royces and life-size effigies of servants and mistresses.

AFTER DEATH, the spirits need a fiery contribution of cash, especially during the annual Hungry Ghosts Festival on the first day of the seventh moon. For two weeks the gateway to hell is opened and the ghosts come forth, free to walk the earth, and in need of cash and a good meal. Their living relatives prepare a feast for them and burn hell money to keep them happy – after all, if they're not happy all hell could break loose! }

FENG SHUI*

{ *** FENG SHUI IS BIG BUSINESS IN HONG KONG. LITERALLY MEANING 'WIND AND WATER', THE SCIENCE** (or art, depending on who you believe) of balance and placement is applied to architecture throughout the city, but is most noticeable in the towers of Hong Kong Island. }

AMONG THE MORE obvious examples of feng shui in action is the HSBC Main Building, designed by British architect Sir Norman Foster in 1985. Not only are there open spaces throughout it, there's also an all-important water view, which the government is reputed to be protecting by refusing building permission in front of the tower. It's a theory that seems to have been borne out – no new buildings have gone up in the huge redevelopment of the Central waterfront.

URBAN LEGEND also suggests that the unfeasibly large window-cleaning winches pointing from the roof of the HSBC building toward the nearby Bank of China Tower are there to ward off that tower's bad feng shui.

40.

FORTUNATE ONES *

*IN A CITY WHERE LUCK, MONEY AND RELIGION ARE INSEPARABLE, WONG TAI SIN TEMPLE IS HONG KONG'S ONE-STOP LUCK SUPERMARKET.** Below the main temple dedicated to the god Wong Tai Sin (who is able to cure all illnesses) is an arcade filled with fortune-tellers. Here Hong Kongers consult their choice of more than 100 soothsayers. For a fee, these wise ones can divine the future by reading your palm – or by reading something more exotic, such as the chim (fortune sticks) or sing pei (aka the Buddha's lips). If the signs are positive, then all is good. If not, fear not: Hong Kong is a land of positive fatalism where no fate is beyond change. All that's required is belief, and a bit more money.

BEHIND THE MAIN temple are the Good Wish Gardens, where zigzag bridges join waterfalls, lakes and carp ponds. Among the gardens' colourful pavilions is the very beautiful Unicorn Hall, known for its carved doors and windows.

43.

MAN MO TEMPLE*

*THIS BUSY 18TH-CENTURY TEMPLE, SQUATTING LOW BENEATH THE CONCRETE TOWERS, IS ONE OF THE OLDEST AND MOST FAMOUS IN HONG KONG. Literally meaning 'civil and military', the Man Mo Temple is a shrine to two deities: Man Cheung, an ancient Chinese statesman who is worshipped as the god of literature, and Kwan Tai, a soldier born in the second century AD who is venerated as the red-cheeked god of war. (Man Cheung is represented holding a writing brush; Kwan Tai holds a sword.) Kwan Tai has additional status as the patron god of restaurants, pawnshops, the police force and secret societies such as the Triads.

THE MAN MO TEMPLE is an odd place of worship: a couple of times a year its incense-scented interior hosts a rather eccentric gathering. Because Kwan Tai is the patron god of both the police and Triad gangsters, these archenemies are forced to tolerate each other's presence when paying tribute to him.

45.

SQUISHY SQUASHY*

{ *** ALMOST EVERYONE IN HONG KONG LIVES IN AN APARTMENT,** whether it's a 450-square-metre place with expansive views from exclusive Victoria Peak (for a cool HK$125,000 a month) or a 22.5-square-metre shoebox in the New Territories (for HK$2,000 a month). }

WHILE THE SKYLINE is impressive by day, it's after the sun goes down that you begin to feel how truly exotic this sort of existence can be. Sitting at the window looking out is like watching hundreds of silent movies being played simultaneously – it's the neighbours. The square boxes of light in the towers around allow glimpses into a thousand lives. They're usually mundane, but always fascinating.

GROWING UP in such an environment does have its effects. For example, Hong Kongers will almost never get naked while the curtains or blinds are open: you just don't do that. And many don't have a drivers licence, because not only are cars expensive to run, they're pricey to park as well.

46.

HONG KONG WAS once a lair for pirates and smugglers. It was ceded to the British in 1842; treaties in 1860 and 1898 granted it more territory, and its population increased from 33,000 in 1850 to 265,000 in 1900. These days most Hong Kongers live close to their neighbours – there are a suffocating 50,820 people living in one square kilometre at Kwun Tong in New Kowloon. It's here that the stereo-typical Hong Kong lifestyle is most evident, the young people playing mah jong with their grandparents, while constantly checking their new mobile phones for text messages.

TAI CHI*

{ *EVERY MORNING TAI CHI CHUAN, THE 'GRAND ULTIMATE FIST', IS PRACTISED IN PARKS, STREETS AND ON BALCONIES ACROSS HONG KONG.** The stylised shadow-boxing could be moves from some slow-motion kung fu movie – you half expect Jackie Chan to come flying, in slo-mo of course, out from behind a tree and be effortlessly brushed aside by a septuagenarian performing the classic Step Back and Repulse Monkey. }

MORE SERIOUSLY, though, tai chi is about health and inner peace. It's a terrific form of exercise, improving muscle tone, developing breathing muscles and promoting good health in general. It's also a solid foundation for other martial arts that were traditionally passed down through the generations. They were seldom taught to outsiders, as the skills were considered far too valuable to spread indiscriminately.

51.

TAKE THE SLOW BOAT *

TAKING TO THE HARBOUR IN A TINY SAMPAN AFTER MIDNIGHT, AS IT ROCKS AND ROLLS ACROSS THE WAVES between the dark shapes of container ships, Macau-bound ferries and other hulking sea craft, is so James Bond… and so Hong Kong. Long before fast ferries and hydrofoils, these round-nosed boats were the main means of travel between the islands. They are usually family-run, with mum often taking the helm while dad keeps the motor running. Although sampans have been largely replaced by bigger ferries for passenger traffic, there are still plenty around, sometimes taking on the role of removalist, loaded full of furnishings for a trip from Aberdeen to Lamma or Cheung Chau island.

MORE DISTINCTIVE and exciting are the long, thin dragon boats brought out at the Dragon Boat Festival in May or June. Colourful and noisy with drumbeats and voices, they're raced in the waters off Stanley, watched from the shore, from boats and on TV. The uproar is enough to frighten off the fishes, which is appropriate given that the festival commemorates the efforts of locals to rescue the corpse of drowned national hero Qu Yuan in the 3rd century BC.

53.

CHEONGSAM *

{ *** VERY FEW EXPRESSIONS OF CHINESE BEAUTY ARE AS COMPLETE AS THE CHEONGSAM,** the closest thing Hong Kong has to national dress. The close-fitting, floor-length dress is the epitome of elegant sexiness: always alluring but never unseemly, and the thigh-high slits up the sides have a tendency to turn heads. }

THIS BEDAZZLING dress started as a man's garment during the Qing dynasty. In the 1920s, women in Shanghai liked it so much they took to wearing a similar garment – until it was banned during the Cultural Revolution.

THE CHEONGSAM had no such trouble in Hong Kong, where it reigned supreme during the 1950s and '60s and was brought to the world's attention by the film *The World of Suzie Wong*. These days it's harder to spot on the streets, though virtually every Hong Kong woman (and more than a few men) has one in the wardrobe for that special occasion. Modern Hong Kong brides may take their vows in white, but to slip away for the honeymoon they put on a red cheongsam.

DELICIOUS*

{ ***IT'S NO ACCIDENT THAT HONG KONG HAS BECOME ONE OF THE WORLD'S GREAT FOOD CITIES.** To understand the outcome, just look at the ingredients. The Cantonese love food; they will eat 'anything with its back to the sky' and 'anything underwater except a submarine'; the British made Hong Kong an international place, attracting cuisines from around China and the world; Hong Kongers love money, so there is always enough around to reward the best chefs and the most entrepreneurial and imaginative restaurateurs; and eating is central to Chinese social interaction, whether for business or leisure. }

STIR FRY THIS in the wok of history for 165 years and the result becomes an eating destination hard to top. Not surprisingly, Cantonese cuisine is the city's favourite. Whether it's a family dim sum meal on a Sunday morning, a plate of double-boiled wild duck with deer's penis and gecko in a 'health' restaurant, or a simple dish of fresh vegetables in a dai pai dong, the range is astonishing.

BUT THERE'S MORE on offer than Cantonese fare – the city is a living database of Chinese food. Garlic-fuelled Chiu Chow cuisine is popular, as are the stewed and braised Shanghainese dishes and the steamed bread, dumplings and mutton in Northern Chinese eateries. The sophistication of modern Hong Kong can be summed up in a meal at a sleek stainless-steel Sichuan place – delight in nine courses of pure fire then see the chef emerge to sing Chinese opera. Sublime!

IN DISTRICTS like SoHo the evidence of Hong Kong's rapidly maturing palate is plain to see. Where once the French, Italian, Argentinean, Nepalese, Indian, Australian, Spanish, Japanese, Greek, Russian, Mexican and Chinese restaurants (phew!) were filled with wealthy young expats, these days they're often outnumbered by Chuppies (Chinese yuppies). Eating international cuisines has become pretty hip.

WHERE YOU EAT is almost as important, and Hong Kong has some fantastic tables with a view. Even so, few restaurants on earth have a panorama to beat Felix, on the top two floors of Hong Kong's 'grand dame', the Peninsula Hotel. It's here that Philippe Starck's combination of aluminium, Art Deco and moody lighting taps into the city's view of itself as a chic sophisticate. But it's the view that will stop your heart. From the Peninsula Hotel's fleet of green Rolls Royces parked below, across the bobbing lights on Victoria Harbour and on to the neon jungle of Central and Wan Chai, it's a magnet for the eyes.

HONG KONG'S culinary scene is both created by and vital to its collective personality, and is well summed up in an old Chinese proverb: 'Good fortune of the mouth is no mean thing'. Hong Kongers haven't left it to luck – they've made sure that where the mouth is concerned, they are very fortunate indeed.

DIM SUM*

*THE CLASSIC CANTONESE FOOD, DIM SUM, IS A FAVOURITE SOCIAL DINING EXPERIENCE FOR HONG KONGERS**, who congregate in tiny restaurants or vast halls to eat it for breakfast, brunch or lunch.

LITERALLY, DIM SUM means 'to touch the heart', but it's generally understood to be a 'snack'… usually a rather large snack. There are thought to be more than 1000 different dim sum dishes, most of which are savoury offerings steamed in small bamboo baskets, though typically only about 30 or 40 of these will be available. In older-style places the baskets are stacked onto carts and pushed between tables, where diners inspect and select dishes to share with their group. But in most modern restaurants ordering is done from a tick-a-box menu.

THE ACT OF EATING dim sum is usually referred to as yum cha, which means 'drink tea' in Cantonese, as all the dishes are washed down with never-ending pots of tea.

61.

DAI PAI DONG*

{ *PERHAPS HONG KONG'S MOST CHARISMATIC EATERIES ARE DAI PAI DONG, }
literally 'big licence food stall' after the large sheet on which the licences were once
printed. Dai pai dong were traditionally small independent operators hawking dishes
such as snails or chilli mudcrabs. They were the masters of their own destiny, in true
Hong Kong style.

THESE DAYS, however, overly cautious bureaucrats have driven most dai pai dong
operators into licensed areas. These often comprise dozens of kitchens in vast spaces
above wet markets, serving cheap seafood accompanied by a free-flowing supply of
beer. Man Yuen, a dai pai dong that sold noodles for 80 years, saw hundreds flocking
to have a last bowl of noodles on its closing day recently.

A MODERN VERSION of a dai pai dong in Canton Road serves meals throughout the
day, including such oddities as white coffee with equal parts of black tea, and toast
smeared with condensed milk.

BIRD'S NEST SOUP*

{ *THE CANTONESE BELIEVE SOUP IS A VITAL INGREDIENT IN ANY MEAL AND THAT PARTICULAR INGREDIENTS BRING BALANCE TO THE BODY.** It gives you heat in winter and cools you in summer. Traditionally, it was the beverage component of the meal (a role it now shares with drinks), and one of the last courses served at a banquet. }

WON TON SOUP is perhaps the most well-known broth, but Hong Kongers also have a thing for more exotic soups. Snakes often end up in the pot, as do deers' penises and an ever-growing number of sharks' fins, which are believed to be an aphrodisiac for men and the secret to a beautiful complexion for women. (For the endangered sharks, of course, it just means death.)

BUT IT'S YIN WOH GENG, or bird's nest soup, that Westerners find hardest to understand. It's an expensive delicacy, and making the soup involves slowly steaming and soaking birds' nests, often for several days. And the benefit… longer life, of course.

64.

NOODLES ARE THOUGHT to have originated in northern China during the Han dynasty, when the Chinese developed techniques for the large-scale grinding of flour. Legend credits Marco Polo with taking noodles to Italy in 1295. In Hong Kong, fried noodles are the most popular but by no means the only type on offer. There are also thin, translucent strands of mung bean starch; wide, white, flat, slippery rice noodles; yellow balls of twine-like noodles; and won ton noodles with duck egg, to name a small selection. In some places you can still have the mesmeric joy of watching the dough rolled and stretched, folded and pulled until, just like that, you have noodles.

CHEAP EATS*

{ ***LIKE A SCENE OUT OF *BLADE RUNNER*, WITH DIRTY ALLEYS, BETEL NUT–STAINED WALLS, FLICKERING NEON TUBES AND AN ARRAY OF MIGRANTS** in search of a cheap bed or a fast buck, Chungking Mansions is the ugly face of Hong Kong. Take a room for the night and your bed will be a bench that squeezes between the walls and the 'ensuite' a toilet at the end of the bed with a showerhead above to clean you and the toilet at the same time. }

BUT WHILE THESE dilapidated blocks are infamous for their cheap and charmless hotels, they're also home to some of the city's best Indian and Pakistani restaurants. Small, cheap and sometimes illegal, these places are often no more than a two-room apartment with a couple of tables, an improvised kitchen and a television playing Bollywood films or cricket. At first glance it might seem too grimy, but in several established places the grotty exteriors open into plush (if somewhat claustrophobic) dining areas, with soft lights, soft Indian music and nary a television to be seen. Then there's the food, which is inspired.

EATING ETIQUETTE*

HONG KONGERS AREN'T OVERLY HUNG UP ON EATING ETIQUETTE, BUT EVEN THE MOST ILL-MANNERED WOULD NEVER LEAVE THEIR CHOPSTICKS standing in a bowl of rice, because the similarity of this to incense sticks in a bowl of ashes makes it a sign of death. Equally, you won't see diners flipping their fish to get to the meat on the bottom, as this guarantees the next fishing boat they pass will capsize. On the other hand, a tablecloth splattered with food is perfectly acceptable – it means you enjoyed your meal.

WHEN HONG KONGERS get together it's almost always in a restaurant. Whether for a family get-together or a billion-dollar business lunch, an eatery that will impress the guests and bring good 'face' to the host is the preferred choice. The host will often insist on paying and the wise guest will graciously accept, lest the host incur a serious loss of face.

ESCAPIST*

{ ***IF HONG KONG IS LIKE A CITY ON SPEED, IT'S THE POSSIBILITY OF ESCAPE THAT KEEPS IT SANE.** With seven million people living in just 10% of the city's area, coming down with 'island fever' is a very real possibility. Thankfully, the cure is near. That other 90% of the island is at once an escapologist's dream and an unequivocal rebuttal of the idea that the only jungle in Hong Kong is made of concrete. Knowing escape is so near provides Hong Kongers, and the city as a whole, with a critical release valve when urban reality becomes too much. }

FROM A PRACTICAL point of view, the city is the envy of most of its contemporaries because getting out of the rat race is so simple. From the epicentre of the financial district in Central you can rise above it all on the Peak Tram or hop on the Star Ferry, both within a few minutes of deciding you need to be out of there.

VENTURE A LITTLE further from frenetic Central and you'll find a city of enchanting contradictions. Whether it's atmospheric lanes on Cheung Chau, deserted beaches on

73.

uninhabited islands known only to your friendly junk captain, hiking trails crisscrossing Lantau and the hills of the New Territories, or the car-free counterculture of Lamma, Hong Kong's escapes are all within a few kilometres of the city centre.

NOT ALL ESCAPES involve fleeing the urban chaos, though. Consider those greying Chinese gentlemen in pyjamas slowly practising tai chi as the dawn light struggles through the mist. Maybe they'll startle a monkey and watch it dashing out of the subtropical jungle that clings to the mountain. This might sound like one of Hong Kong's distant islands, but it's not. It's the lower reaches of Victoria Peak, where narrow streets wind through the trees, and cars are few and far between. And it's less than 500 metres from the heart of Central. An even greater contrast can be found in the Kowloon Walled City, which is completely surrounded by urban madness. And it's all free. For context, think how far you'd need to travel from the heart of London, New York or Paris before you found similar escapes, and think of doing it on public transport…

OF COURSE not everyone wants to get sweaty. There remains a sizable number of Hong Kongers for whom the very idea of physical exercise is enough to send them straight to the massage table. They are served by a multitude of spas, massage studios and acupuncturists that can rub, prick, pummel and pamper stress to the furthest corners of the mind. But this is Hong Kong, so taking a well-endowed wallet is wise.

STAR FERRY*

{

* IT'S HARD TO IMAGINE THAT A SEVEN-MINUTE TRIP BETWEEN BUSTLING KOWLOON AND EVEN-MORE-BUSTLING CENTRAL can be much of a change of pace. But it is. The Star Ferry service, its ageing wooden ferries bearing names like *Celestial Star* and *Twinkling Star*, is like a tonic for tired souls. Sitting on the wooden seats on a clear night, the groan of the teak floor mixing with the drone of the engine and salty air rustling your hair as the ferry draws slowly toward the neon skyline of Central, is a sensory recharge that's pure Hong Kong.

THE STAR FERRY service began operating in about 1888, sailing every day except Monday and Friday, when the ferries were used for coal delivery. During the Japanese invasion, the ferries were used to evacuate refugees and Allied troops from Kowloon to Hong Kong Island. It remained the only way to cross the harbour until the Cross-Harbour Tunnel opened in 1978 and the first of the MTR lines began operating in 1980. Today, it remains a much-loved Hong Kong institution… and a great escape.

TRAILING*

HONG KONG AND LANTAU ISLANDS AND THE NEW TERRITORIES ARE CRISS-CROSSED WITH HIKING TRAILS. The Dragon's Back trail follows a mountain ridge at the east end of Hong Kong Island and appeals to those wanting to exercise the legs first and the taste buds later – near the end of the track is the delightful beach village of Shek O, with its low-key bars and restaurants.

THE MACLEHOSE TRAIL is a different story. The full trail is 100 kilometres of panoramic views and pain that winds its way around the New Territories – it was once used by Britain's famed Gurkha soldiers to keep fit. The only food available is what you carry with you, so you feel in the middle of nowhere despite being in one of the most densely populated cities on earth.

FOR A HIKE on the city's doorstep, take a morning walk along Central's narrow lanes to the streets that hug The Peak. As the mist clears over the jasmine and wax trees the glass towers of Admiralty will be revealed, almost level with the eye.

79.

LAMMA ISLAND*

{ * **LAMMA IS ONE OF HONG KONG'S EASIEST GETAWAYS.** The territory's third-largest }
island is a leisurely half-hour ferry ride from Central, but feels – yes, you know what's
coming – a world away from the hustle and bustle. And it is. There's something of a
bohemian feel to Lamma, especially in the main village of Yung Shue Wan, which is
home to writers, artists, musicians and unreconstructed hippies. The hills above the
village are strewn with small homes and apartment blocks. It's home, too, to many
fisherfolk, which makes for some excellent seafood dinners. But it's the complete lack
of cars that really makes it special. No cars means an easy stroll to the famous fish
restaurants of Sok Kwu Wan.

THE GREEN TURTLES that like to nest on the southwest coast are not so concerned
about cars, but their lives are certainly threatened – the water as well as the air of the
city is polluted, and turtles are more likely to be seen on plates than in the wild.
Fortunately, the Hong Kong government has set aside one of Lamma's beautiful beaches for the turtles, who struggle onto the sand to lay their eggs here every year.

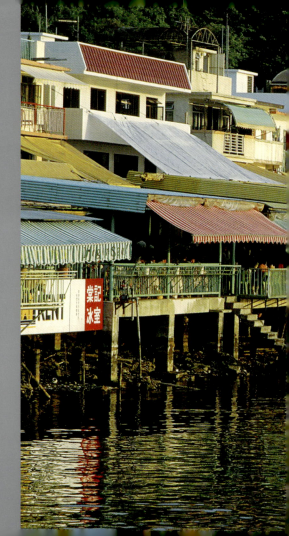

GETTING BACK TO Hong Kong Island from Sok Kwu Wan on Lamma Island is an escape in itself, especially if you engage a sampan. In that case the journey usually begins with some bargaining, probably with a middle-aged woman who looks like she'd take no prisoners. With the fee settled, she'll load you on and ship you out onto the South China Sea. It's not such a long trip to Aberdeen, but it's a whole lot of fun.

PARK LIFE *

{ *** NESTLED IN KOWLOON, THE WALLED CITY PARK REFLECTS AT ONCE THE EXOTIC AND ESCAPIST SIDES OF THE HONG KONG PERSONALITY.** The park was originally a garrison, with a yamen (commander's office) to represent the power of the emperor as passed down to the mandarin in charge of the fort. }

UNTIL 1984 the area inside the walls remained part of China, as it had been omitted from the 1898 lease of the New Territories. Ungoverned by Britain but cut off from China, it was infamous for its gangsters, gambling, prostitution and – brace yourself – illegal dentists.

WHEN THE BRITISH finally acquired the village, they moved the residents out and transformed it into a beautiful urban park filled with plants, pavilions and ponds full of turtles and goldfish. The exquisite trees and shrubs include a long hedge that's been coaxed into the form of a dragon. The yamen, one of the few remaining in China, has been restored, and there are remnants of two original gates, plus two cannons.

85.

PIRATE ISLAND *

{ * **TINY CHEUNG CHAU ISLAND HAS BEEN USED AS A BOLT HOLE SINCE PIRATES AND SMUGGLERS HID OUT HERE CENTURIES AGO,** preying on passing ships. The infamous 18th-century pirate Cheung Po Tsai was based here, and stashed his loot in a cave at the southwestern tip of the island. }

THESE DAYS Cheung Chau is one of the last places in Hong Kong where people live on wooden junks. The number falls year by year, but there are still quite a few families for whom home is where they drop their anchor.

CHEUNG CHAU IS also the home of the Bun Festival, a Taoist celebration for the god Pak Tai. The Bun Festival celebrations include building tall bamboo towers covered with white buns, each bearing a red stamp. Traditionally the festival would culminate with people scrambling up the towers to grab the buns for luck – the higher the bun, the better the luck. A vigorous bun fight in 1978 brought a tower down, however, and the tradition was halted. Happily, it resumed in 2005 using aluminium frames and safety harnesses.

86.

90.

GOLD STAR

A GOLD STAR TO HONG KONG FOR ENTREPRENEURIAL SPIRIT – WHATEVER THE DEMAND, SOMEONE IS THERE TO SUPPLY IT. WHETHER IT'S A HUMBLE DAI PAI DONG DINNER, ELECTRONIC EQUIPMENT, LINGERIE OR A NIGHTLIFE THAT NEVER ENDS, YOU'LL FIND WHAT YOU WANT IN HONG KONG.

MY PERFECT DAY

ANDREW BURKE

{ * Start the day with an early morning walk around The Peak, taking in the tai chi and soaking up the city as it wakes. Head back through Mid-Levels and stop in SoHo for a coffee before stepping into the urgency of peak-hour Central. Elbow your way (go on, don't be shy) across to the Bank of China Tower for the awesome views from the 43rd floor, and skip across to City Hall to join hundreds of chattering locals for a delicious dim sum breakfast at Maxim's. Suitably fortified, take the ferry to Lamma Island for a taste of Hong Kong's escapist side. Walk from Yung Shue Wan to tiny Sok Kwu Wan for a delicious seafood lunch, then unleash your adventurous side and jump on a sampan to Aberdeen, for an unforgettably romantic Hong Kong experience.

Take the bus back to Central and from there the Star Ferry at sunset to Tsim Shu Tsui, for a sample of the two extremes of Hong Kong. First, sip a cocktail, gawp at the views and experience the city at its most stylish in the Peninsula Hotel's Felix bar, then head around the corner to grungy Chungking Mansions for a dirt-cheap curry. Still kicking? Get down to Lan Kwai Fong.

}

ANDREW BURKE IS A WRITER AND PHOTOGRAPHER WHO HAS SPENT MUCH OF THE LAST DECADE LIVING AND WORKING IN ASIA. That time has included three years in Hong Kong, much of which was spent working for the *South China Morning Post* newspaper. His time in Hong Kong has left Andrew with a deep affection for the city state and the people who live there, and he travels back at least once a year. Andrew has worked as a journalist and photographer for newspapers for more than 15 years, and has written and contributed to several travel guides for Lonely Planet, including *China*, *Laos* and *Iran*. He now lives in Cambodia with his wife, Anne.

PHOTO CREDITS

}

CITIESCAPE
HONG KONG

OCTOBER 2006

**PUBLISHED BY LONELY PLANET
PUBLICATIONS PTY LTD**
ABN 36 005 607 983
90 Maribyrnong St, Footscray,
Victoria 3011, Australia
www.lonelyplanet.com

Printed through Colorcraft Ltd, Hong Kong.
Printed in China.

PHOTOGRAPHS
Many of the images in this book are available
for licensing from Lonely Planet Images.
www.lonelyplanetimages.com

ISBN 1 74104 935 0

© Lonely Planet 2006
© photographers as indicated 2006

LONELY PLANET OFFICES
AUSTRALIA Locked Bag 1, Footscray, Victoria 3011
Telephone 03 8379 8000 Fax 03 8379 8111
Email talk2us@lonelyplanet.com.au

USA 150 Linden St, Oakland, CA 94607
Telephone 510 893 8555 TOLL FREE 800 275 8555
Fax 510 893 8572 Email info@lonelyplanet.com

UK 72–82 Rosebery Ave, London EC1R 4RW
Telephone 020 7841 9000 Fax 020 7841 9001
Email go@lonelyplanet.co.uk

Publisher ROZ HOPKINS
Commissioning Editor ELLIE COBB
Editors JOCELYN HAREWOOD, VANESSA BATTERSBY
Design MARK ADAMS
Layout Designer INDRA KILFOYLE
Image Researcher PEPI BLUCK
Pre-press Production GERARD WALKER
Project Managers ANNELIES MERTENS, ADAM MCCROW
Publishing Planning Manager JO VRACA
Print Production Manager GRAHAM IMESON